JOURNEYS THROUGH AMERICAN HISTORY

Volume I: Native Americans and Revolutionary Times

By James T. Parks

We all owe a debt of gratitude to those intrepid souls who came before us; they forged the remarkable history of what became, and is, the United States of America—thank you! As we travel through America's past and present, let us continue learning from and preserving the richness of our country's incomparable parklands, iconic landscapes, historic places, diverse human cultures, and sacred sites. Of course, I would also like to thank my wife, Karen, for putting up with my many long hours spent on this project.

Journeys Through American History

This book is the first volume of a collection of *RoadRUNNER* travelogues written by James T. Parks, which focus on locations and routes steeped in American history. Jim's original articles are scattered piecemeal throughout various *RoadRUNNER* bimonthly issues, spanning more than a decade of time. With that in mind, we have updated information, where feasible, that appeared in the original articles. Readers, who are interested in how America came to be what it is today, will find this integrated collection of historically themed adventures of particular interest, regardless of your mode of transportation.

Volume I focuses on Native American history and several revolutionary events that helped win our independence and build America's industrial might. Come along with us and enjoy these journeys through American history.

Christa Neuhauser
Publisher & Editor-in-Chief
RoadRUNNER Motorcycle Touring & Travel magazine

© 2020 by RoadRUNNER Publishing division of European Creative Communication Inc.

ISBN: 978-1513660165 (paperback)

Library in Congress Cataloging-in-Publication Data

Journey's Through American History, Vol. 1, James T. Parks

Printed in USA

Photography: James T. Parks, RoadRUNNER Publishing

First printing: March 2020

TABLE OF CONTENTS

PALEO AMERICA:

Before the arrival of Europeans, America was already inhabited by tribes of indigenous people in its various regions. The following article describes a modern-day trip through one of those regions, looking back many centuries.

A COLORADO PLATEAU ODYSSEY IN AMERICA'S FOUR CORNERS REGION

It's early September and the summer tourists have abandoned the 130,000-square-mile red rock landscape known by geologists as the Colorado Plateau. It contains the largest concentration of scenic wonders in America. Roughly centered where the states of New Mexico, Colorado, Utah and Arizona meet, the plateau was once home to the Anasazi, a largely vanished Native American culture that began living in this arid environment as early as 1200 B.C. The prospect of seeing archeological remnants of these ancient Puebloan people promises to make this trip an unforgettable adventure.

THE COLORADO PLATEAU

Hundreds of millions of years ago, shallow seas deposited layers of sediment several miles thick. Over the eons the seas receded and those sedimentary layers were forced deep into the earth where intense heat and pressure fused them into rock. Later, tectonic plate movement caused the entire western US to begin rising some 5-to-10 million years ago, forming the Rocky and Sierra Nevada mountain ranges. But the thick rocky crust of the Colorado Plateau didn't bend and fold from those forces. Instead, it was uplifted largely intact and then eroded into the dramatic red rock landscape we see today.

From Cuba, NM, my nephew Steve Brown and I travel northwest into an enormous landscape that's largely devoid of modern civilization. A thin ribbon of two-lane asphalt snaking its way across the plateau seems a tenuous human lifeline in this world of stone. Although the temperature is in the 80s, the combination of very low humidity and an altitude ranging from 6,000-to-7,000 feet makes travel and on-foot discovery quite comfortable. The feeling is both exhilarating and humbling, out here where the colossal forces of nature rule over mankind.

INTO CHACO CANYON

At the turn-off from US 550 to Chaco Culture National Historical Park, a sign indicates that there's no food, gas, or hotels from here on. All but 8 miles of this 21-mile road are dirt and gravel. We fly over the rutted-out, washboard roadway, and splash through a shallow water crossing, sending spray onto the dry desert surface. Then, the road subtly winds its way onto a dry wash canyon floor and we're soon surrounded by Chaco Canyon.

Chaco Culture National Historical Park has one of the most extraordinary collections of ancient ruins north of Mexico. The park's mission is to carefully manage the exploration and preservation of these ancient dwellings.

At the Visitors Center we learn that Chaco Canyon was the cultural center of an agriculturally based civilization. The Anasazi, who lived here, were expert dry land farmers. This Pueblo culture was at its zenith between A.D. 900 to 1100. A 400-mile network of roads straight-as-an-arrow connected Chaco to over 75 outlying Pueblo villages.

The distinctive black and white pottery excavated here is the signature archeological marker of Chacoan culture. The fine craftsmanship exhibited by the ruins makes it clear that the former residents were master stonemasons. But something happened here in the 12th century that caused the residents of Chaco Canyon to abandon their homes. Archeologists have a variety of theories, but no one knows for sure why they left.

CHANGING SKIES

We hike to Richard Wetherill's gravesite and contemplate the curious life of this cowboy turned archeologist. It would be easy to spend a whole day visiting the ancient dwellings in Chaco Canyon, but we notice a dark specter on the horizon. A distant thunderstorm is pummeling the arid terrain with sheets of rain and jagged bolts of lightning. The storm is headed our way.

Although still miles away, the storm could trigger a flash flood that turns the shallow water crossing into a raging torrent on the road out of Chaco Canyon. Although the water is still shallow at the crossing, the tempest finally catches us on US 550. Hard rain turns into bullets of hail. In Bloomfield, NM, our overnight destination, the skies suddenly clear; thankfully, Mother Nature's rolling rampage has moved on.

A SHIP MADE OF ROCK

"I'm not sure Steve," I mutter, "do you think it looks like a ship?"

"Maybe it does from a different angle," he replies.

Shiprock's jagged black peak, thrusting 1,800 feet above the high plains of the Navajo Indian Reservation, is a breathtaking sight to behold. This massive rock formation is the core of an ancient volcano that's been dormant for around 30 million years.

Wind and water eroded the softer sedimentary rock that originally surrounded it, leaving six volcanic dykes radiating from the towering summit. In some directions Shiprock can be seen from 100 miles away.

Because Shiprock lies on Navajo land and is a sacred place for the Navajo people, we view it from a distance. The spiritual world of Native Americans is very different from that perceived by descendents of European culture. The Navajo and other Native Americans usually have an enduring bond with their sacred places. The spirits of their ancestors are believed to reside in many of the iconic mountains, mesas, buttes, spires, canyons, and pueblo ruins on the Colorado Plateau. While non-Native people may find these places to be curious remnants of the past, they are very much alive to Native Americans.

CANYONS IN THE SKY

Seemingly mature people are doing all sorts of calisthenics in four states at once, while others gleefully photograph their contortions. The Four Corners Monument, the only place in the US where four states touch, is one of those geographical anomalies that we travelers find so irresistible.

In southwest Colorado we're working our way along the base of a massive, high mesa that dominates our view to the east. I wonder about this enormous island in the sky, not yet realizing that it's the western wall of Mesa Verde. The imposing landscape we're exploring is exciting, spiritual, and overpowering— all at the same time.

Arriving in Cortez, CO, at noon on a Sunday, we notice that the place is crawling with tourists. They are obviously out enjoying the many sights of scenic splendor in the mild September weather. Our stomachs are growling rather loudly, so we stop in town for a quick repast in a small cafe. With appetites satiated, we head east to explore the wonders of Mesa Verde's canyons in the sky.

Mesa Verde, which is Spanish for green table, was the home of Ancestral Puebloans (or Anasazi) people from A.D. 600 to 1300. The 81-square-mile Mesa Verde National Park protects over 4,000 known archeological sites, which are among the best preserved in the US.

The altitude on top of the mesa rises to 8,400 feet and is dissected by vertiginous canyons, running north and south. Paved, two-lane roads curve gracefully up and down the imposing but stunning terrain.

Only a few of the cliff dwellings built within caves and outcroppings in cliffs are open to the public. A well-marked path leads us down a shallow canyon to the Spruce Tree House cliff dwelling. One of the kivas, which were the ceremonial gathering places for residents, has a restored roof with the top of a ladder protruding through a small portal. Only the adventurous squeeze through the opening and climb down the ladder to contemplate the kiva's dark interior. (Note: Spruce Tree House has been closed for several years to stabilize some of the interior rock surfaces but should reopen before too long.)

ANASAZI
WHAT'S IN A NAME?

The name Anasazi comes from a Navajo word that was first applied to the ancient inhabitants of the Mesa Verde ruins by Richard Wetherill. The Navajo meaning for Anasazi, however, is something on the order of "enemy ancestor." As prominent archeologists began exploring ancient ruins on the Colorado Plateau, Anasazi became their preferred shorthand name for these ancient Puebloans, over a more technical term. Some of the modern descendents of this culture, most notably the Hopi Indians, use the word Hisatsinom (or Pueblo People).

Because there is no agreement among modern-day Native American tribes on the proper name, some archeologists continue to use Anasazi. The National Park Service uses the more politically correct name "Ancestral Puebloans" in their literature about the various national parks and monuments that they administer. Since this tour has an archeology focus, we often use the name "Anasazi."

In stark contrast to Chaco Canyon and earlier villages on top of Mesa Verde, these 12th- and 13th-century cliff dwellings reflect a trend towards a far denser concentration of people into closer, more defensible quarters. The design of these structures, combined with the sudden departure of the Anasazi residents around A.D. 1275, leaves us wondering why they left.

ACROSS THE SAGEBRUSH PLAIN
Monday morning's cloudless sky foretells another beautiful day on the Colorado Plateau. We head north to McPhee Reservoir, which is the second largest man-made body of water in Colorado. It was constructed to provide irrigation for farming of the otherwise dry sagebrush plain. Nearby, we stop at a museum that is home to an extensive collection of Native American artifacts.

 The Anasazi Heritage Center, which manages a collection of about 3 million items, is dedicated to the Anasazi and other Native American cultures in the Four Corners region. Exhibits include superb displays of prehistoric Native American pottery and other artifacts, most of which were excavated from 120 archeological sites during the construction of nearby McPhee Reservoir.

The sun is getting high as we journey across Colorado's arid, featureless Sagebrush Plain. Incredibly, the Anasazi also lived in this particularly inhospitable region. Although there is no welcome sign to greet us, my GPS indicates that we've finally arrived in the state of Utah, where our Anasazi archeological adventure continues.

The modern-day popular media have sometimes portrayed the Anasazi people as having mysteriously vanished without a trace. Some have even implied that there is a paranormal or extraterrestrial explanation for their "sudden" disappearance. In our quest to better understand a more earthly explanation for the Anasazi's disappearance, Steve and I continue our adventure, along the Trail of the Ancients National Scenic Byway, in the remote southeast corner of Utah.

NAVAJO NATION
Our first stop in Utah is at Anasazi ruins with dwellings that are noticeably different from anything we've seen so far. Hovenweep National Monument is the site of six prehistoric Anasazi villages spread over a 20-mile landscape of sage-covered mesas and canyons. Around A.D. 1150 to A.D. 1200, the Anasazi began building larger pueblos combined with fortress-like towers, at the head of box canyons. These structures suggest a defensive style of construction. Archeologists believe that the Anasazi's exodus from this area began in the late 13th century, and evidence suggests that they were the target of vulturous tribes roaming the area.

Heading south we enter the Utah portion of the Navajo Nation. This semi-autonomous Native American homeland, which is the largest of its kind in America, covers more than 27,000 square miles across three states. That's a parcel of land larger than the state of West Virginia. The sagebrush plain gives way to rock-strewn canyons and mesas baking in the noontime sun. In the far distance, we can see canyon walls with shades of red, brown, and tan layered in gigantic geometric patterns that were carved by the enormous erosional forces of the San Juan River.

We stop for lunch at the Twin Peaks Restaurant in Bluff, UT. It's easy to see how both the town and the restaurant got its name: two-towering sandstone spires rise precipitously from a high bluff behind the restaurant. If they ever topple over, the restaurant, as they say, is toast–we eat quickly and depart.

MOTHER NATURE'S MONUMENTS
Millions of people have visited or seen photos of

the incomparable Monument Valley. Relatively few people, though, have had the up-close experience afforded by another stunning valley in the area that's only a quarter of the size of its more famous cousin.

Valley of the Gods, with its tall, red sandstone mesas, buttes and spires rising above the canyon floor, is a small-scale version of Monument Valley. A 16-mile unpaved road winds through spellbinding rock formations that were carved out over many centuries. Utah's Goosenecks State Park overlooks a 1,000-foot deep chasm carved by the San Juan River, meandering back and forth along its sinuous path to the Colorado River. The numerous exposed layers of multi-hued tan sedimentary rock suggest that the river has been long at work creating this scenic

century. They were most likely nomads from much farther north, who moved into a landscape left mostly empty by their Anasazi predecessors.

INCOMPARABLE CANYONS

Bureau of Indian Affairs (BIA) Route 59 is a virtually deserted two-lane road that leads us southeast through more Navajo red rock country. Black Mesa, massive in its proportions, dominates the view to our south. Not many miles beyond that wall of stone is the Hopi Indian Reservation; it's home to a people who believe they are the direct descendents of the ancient Anasazi. Interestingly, the 2,531-square mile Hopi Reservation is completely surrounded by the Navajo Reservation. Arriving in Chinle, AZ, we feel we've been trans-

Chaco Culture National Historical Park has one of the most extraordinary collections of ancient ruins north of Mexico.

wonder. The sun moves lower on the horizon, and we still have another stop on our day's itinerary before sunset.

Monument Valley's iconic sandstone formations resulted from the eroding effects of wind and water in the valley. The scenery has changed little since 1938, when John Ford and John Wayne arrived to film *Stagecoach*. The Monument Valley Navajo Tribal Park maintains a visitor center, campground, and restaurant.

Archeologists believe that a great drought in their northern homelands caused waves of Anasazi to converge in the Kayenta area in the 13th century. Northern Anasazi united with the Kayenta Anasazi, building cliff dwellings with vestiges of the Mesa Verde style of architecture. It's generally believed that the Navajo, the current occupants of this land, didn't arrive in the southwest until around the 16th

ported to another country. And in a way we have, because we're in the heart of the Navajo Nation. A large flea market is going full tilt in a vacant lot. Several unattended cattle mosey down the street. Police drive by in SUVs emblazoned with Navajo signage. A brisk southwestern wind kicks up wisps of red dust, and we seem to be the only Anglos within sight. No doubt the locals are wondering about the two strangers who just got into town.

But we soon discover, over a hearty lunch at the Junction Restaurant, that we're more than welcome to be here, helping the local economy in our own small way. With much daylight still left to burn, we make our way to some of the area's most strikingly beautiful works of nature.

Canyon de Chelly National Monument is one of the longest inhabited landscapes in North America. The monument covers 131 square miles, encompassing the floors and rims of three major canyons: Canyon de Chelly, Canyon del Muerto, and Monument Canyon. These canyon lands sustain a living Navajo community.

Because the afternoon sun illuminates much of Canyon de Chelly's floor and its north wall, we head to South Rim Drive first. Sheer rock walls plunge 600-to-800 feet straight down to the canyon floor. These sandstone cliffs display layers of geological lineage dating back more than 200 million years. A strip of verdant flora reveals the path of Chinle Wash, coursing beneath the canyon floor. Corn and other crops are still grown here by the Navajo.

Access to the canyon floor is restricted. Visitors must be accompanied by a park ranger or an authorized Navajo guide. The White House Ruin Trail, though, is a footpath that hikers are allowed to follow, unaccompanied, to the often-photographed White House cliff dwellings, deep in the canyon. It's a 1½-to-2 hour walk to trek down and back.

The combination of massive red rock cliffs, a luxuriant canyon floor, undiluted sunlight, and small islands of puffy cumulus clouds floating lazily overhead in a cerulean sky, makes this canyon a mesmerizing sight to behold. Its most distinctive geological feature is Spider Rock, a slender sand-

RICHARD WETHERILL (1858-1910)
ARCHEOLOGICAL HERO OR VILLAIN?

When Richard Wetherill, a member of a prominent Colorado ranching family, was rounding up cattle atop Mesa Verde, on December 18, 1888, he first spotted the Cliff Palace ruins. Fascinated by the remains of an ancient society, Wetherill became an amateur archeologist in his explorations of the area. His excavations unearthed a treasure trove of artifacts left by the prehistoric cliff dwellers. In the process, though, walls and roofs were knocked down and other important archeological evidence was disrupted or destroyed.

Later, Wetherill relocated to Chaco Canyon where he homesteaded on land that contained some of the most important Pueblo ruins in the canyon. Wetherill sold many of the artifacts he gathered to museums and he helped other archeologists obtain artifacts from the ruins as well. In contrast to modern archeologists, however, early explorers didn't focus on understanding the people and culture that created the sites. So to protect Mesa Verde from further losses of important archeological information, Congress established Mesa Verde National Park in 1906, the first cultural area set aside within the national park system.

In 1910, while rounding up cattle, Wetherill was ambushed and killed, for reasons that still remain unknown. To some modern archeologists, he remains a villain for his failure to preserve the area he dug up; yet others believe that the knowledge gained from Wetherill's early excavations of Mesa Verde and Chaco Canyon outweighs the damage his explorations inadvertently created. Wetherill's grave is in a small cemetery just west of Pueblo Bonito in Chaco Canyon.

stone spire that soars 800 feet above the junction of Canyon de Chelly and Monument Canyon. With only the faint sound of a gentle wind rustling through pinyon and juniper, these breathtaking vistas encourage quiet contemplation.

To ensure the best light for exploring Canyon del Muerto, we leave early the next morning for North Rim Drive. The hundreds of cliff dwellings, towers and other defensive structures built here by the Anasazi in the 13th century suggests that these canyons were under assault from roaming bands of warring tribes. Excavations have uncovered Anasazi era skeletons that appear to have suffered violent deaths. This Anasazi homeland was occupied only sporadically for the next 400-plus years, until the Navajo began migrating into the canyons.

ZUNI LAND

Gallup, NM is sometimes called the "Indian Capital of the World." But it's also known to historic highway buffs as one of those classic western tourist towns along legendary Route 66. One of its star attractions is the El Rancho Hotel, which has been around since the halcyon days of Route 66. We make it our dinner destination for the evening.

Heading south to the Zuni Indian Reservation from Gallup the next morning, I'm a little sad that it's the last day of our Anasazi adventure. Fortunately, there's one more fascinating archeological site for us to explore before our trip ends. El Morro National Monument, with its waterhole at the base of an imposing sandstone bluff, was a stopping-off place for prehistoric travelers in the area. On top of the bluff are excavated pueblo structures, once occupied by Ancestral Puebloan people for hundreds of years.

Like the Hopi, the Zuni also are believed to be Anasazi descendents. It's eminently clear to us now that the Anasazi didn't just suddenly disappear, as suggested by some. They migrated south, mostly

Excavation of ancient pueblo dwellings atop El Morro National Monument in Cibola County, New Mexico.

along the Rio Grande Valley, to find more plentiful water for growing their crops and to escape the marauding tribes.

At the top of El Morro, we meet a Zuni park ranger who is supervising the excavation and preservation of a network of pueblo structures. He shares some Zuni history with us, including stories of his own ancestors, who lived in the ancient structures being excavated. Marveling at his wonderfully distinctive facial features and long, coal black hair streaming in periodic puffs of wind, I get the unmistakable feeling that the Anasazi are still very much alive here on the Colorado Plateau.

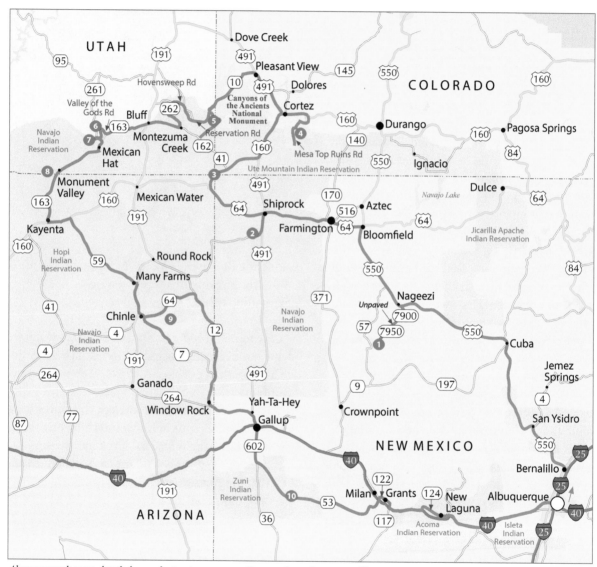

UTAH

95

191

261

Hovensweep Rd

Valley of the
Gods Rd

Bluff

6

163

7

Montezuma
Creek

262

Reservation Rd

Mexican
Hat

Navajo
Indian
Reservation

8

Monument
Valley

163

160

Mexican Water

191

Kayenta

160

Hopi
Indian
Reservation

59

Many Farms

Round Rock

64

41

Chinle

9

4

Navajo
Indian
Reservation

191

7

12

264

Ganado

264

77

Window Rock

87

40

191

ARIZONA

Dove Creek

491

Pleasant View

10

491

Dolores

145

550

COLORADO

160

Canyons of
the Ancients
National
Monument

Cortez

5

160

Durango

160

Pagosa Springs

162

41

160

4

Mesa Top Ruins Rd

140

550

Ignacio

84

3

Ute Mountain Indian Reservation

491

64

Shiprock

170

Navajo Lake

Dulce

64

2

Farmington

516

Aztec

64

64

Bloomfield

Jicarilla Apache
Indian Reservation

84

491

550

371

Nageezi

Unpaved

7900

550

Cuba

57

7950

1

550

Jemez
Springs

9

197

4

Crownpoint

San Ysidro

Yah-Ta-Hey

550

25

Gallup

602

NEW MEXICO

Bernalillo

25

40

Zuni
Indian
Reservation

122

Milan

Grants

124

New
Laguna

Albuquerque

40

10

53

117

Acoma
Indian
Reservation

25

36

40

Isleta
Indian
Reservation

Always consult more-detailed maps for touring purposes. For map legend, see page 65.

FACTS & INFO

FOUR CORNERS REGION

Approximately 700 miles

OVERVIEW

The Four Corners area is a sparsely populated, remote landscape. Food, lodging and fuel stops are not always readily available. Chain hotels are present, though, in Kayenta, Chinle, and Window Rock, AZ, and in Gallup, NM. This tour leads through a stark and stunningly beautiful section of land punctuated with fascinating prehistoric pueblo dwellings. Because of high summer heat, spring and fall are the best times to go.

ROADS

The only unpaved sections in this tour are approximately 13 miles of alternating gravel, hard pack, and sand, on the entrance road to Chaco Canyon, which also includes a shallow water crossing, and about 16 miles of gravel road through the Valley of the Gods. Off-road capable vehicles generally would not be necessary for these roads in dry conditions. The condition of paved roads are generally good-to-excellent.

Download the RoadRUNNER Rides app for turn-by-turn directions.

RESOURCES

- **Colorado Tourism, www.colorado.com**
- **New Mexico Tourism Department** www.newmexico.org
- **Twin Rocks Café, Bluff, UT** www.twinrockscafe.com

POINTS OF INTEREST

1. **Chaco Canyon** www.nps.gov/chcu
2. **Shiprock Geological Formation** Approx. 13 miles SW of Shiprock, NM
3. **Four Corners Monument** www.navajonationparks.org
4. **Mesa Verde National Park** www.nps.gov/meve
5. **Hovenweep National Monument** www.nps.gov/hove
6. **Valley of the Gods** www.tinyurl.com/mon-val-gods
7. **Goosenecks State Park** www.utah.com/goosenecks-state-park
8. **Monument Valley** www.tinyurl.com/monument-val
9. **Canyon de Chelly National Monument** Chinle, AZ, www.nps.gov/cach
10. **El Morro National Monument** www.nps.gov/elmo

AMERICAN REVOLUTION:

Although many of the more famously chronicled Revolutionary War battles were fought in the North, the ones that arguably broke the stalemate and put America on the path to independence took place in the South. This article is about Revolutionary War battles fought in South Carolina.

SOUTH CAROLINA
A REVOLUTIONARY TOUR

By 1780, America's war for its independence from Great Britain had devolved into a stalemate in the northern colonies. British forces controlled major cities on the Atlantic coast, and the Continental Army under George Washington largely dominated the expansive interior. To break the impasse, Britain launched its Southern Strategy: British regulars and colonial Loyalists would subdue the southern colonies and then march north to final victory. Over 200 battles and skirmishes were fought in South Carolina alone, more than in any other colony.

TARLETON GIVES NO QUARTER

Jeff Arpin (my long-time friend and another wandering history buff like me) and I begin our exploration of South Carolina's role in the Revolutionary War by heading to the state's Upcountry, where American Patriots fought bravely to secure our freedoms. Traveling in misty rain, with temperatures in the 50s, I reflect on how the American Revolutionary War

came to South Carolina and the fact that it is often overlooked when the history of our struggle for independence is recounted.

The sky clears as we travel across gently rolling hills, but now we have to dodge logging trucks prevalent in this area. Britain had the world's superior naval force in the 18th century, but it didn't have a massive land army to control large swaths of conquered territory. This primarily explains why Charleston fell after a relatively short siege, but the Brits couldn't subdue armed Patriots in the remote upcountry.

Our first historic site conveys how ardent Loyalist, Captain Christian Huck, was sent by his British commanders to arrest William Bratton. The colonel, who had been leading raids on British outposts, was a constant irritant to the British command. But when Huck and his 130 men arrived at Bratton's house on the evening of July 11, 1780, only his wife was there. When Bratton, who was camped nearby, learned of the British presence, he led a Patriot militia of 500 on a surprise attack the next morning. Captain Huck was killed along with many in his Loyalist force. This Patriot victory earned the sobriquet of Huck's Defeat.

Today, Brattonsville, SC, is a preserved living history museum, containing about thirty 18th and 19th century structures and an interpretive trail through the battlefield. The village's appearance is so authentic that it was used in the movie *The Patriot*, starring Mel Gibson.

Andrew Jackson State Park is located in the same general area as the Battle of Waxhaws, where defeated Patriots were given no "quarter" (reprieve from death) after their surrender to Colonel Banastre Tarleton's British Legion. History is unclear as to whether Tarleton's men committed the white-

GENERAL GATES ABANDONS TROOPS

We travel south over modest elevation changes on mostly straight roads. We're in deep forest following the downstream course of the Catawba River. Not far north of Camden, SC, we pass the Camden Battlefield, where militia forces under General Horatio Gates were routed on August 16, 1780 by a much smaller British force commanded by General Cornwallis and the reviled Tarleton during their march northward into the backcountry.

This military debacle has been ascribed to the strategic ineptitude of Gates, who had formerly been held in high esteem for his role in the Patriots' victory at Saratoga. After his defeat, however, Gates ignominiously abandoned his troops, returning to Continental Army headquarters near Charlotte, NC. General Nathanael Greene replaced Gates the following December, and promptly seized the military initiative in South Carolina.

"Tarleton's Quarter" became a rallying cry for Patriot forces and the hated Tarleton earned the nickname "Bloody Ban."

flagged massacre of Colonel Buford's Virginia Continentals on their own or at Tarleton's behest. Nonetheless, "Tarleton's Quarter" became a rallying cry for Patriot forces and the hated Tarleton earned the nickname "Bloody Ban."

The state park, which is named for our seventh president, has a museum recounting Andrew Jackson's boyhood life in the Waxhaw region. Young Jackson was a witness to two Revolutionary War battles. When he refused, in one encounter, to polish a British officer's boots, the soldier struck Jackson with his sword. The future president's hand partially deflected the blow, saving his life, but the sword left a lifelong scar on the left side of his face.

Founded in 1733, Camden is the oldest inland city in South Carolina. During the Revolutionary War it became a supply depot for British forces. Passing through town, we marvel at the stately plantation-style mansions. Many were built in the early 20th century by wealthy northerners accustomed to fleeing south in the winter.

Motoring farther south in the afternoon, Jeff and I detour slightly from the Revolutionary War to visit Congaree National Park. This 41-square-mile tract preserves the largest area of old growth bottomland hardwood forest remaining in America. Bald cypress trees, with their bulging trunks, are common here. A raised boardwalk charts a round-trip

PERSON OF INTEREST:
GENERAL THOMAS SUMTER (AKA "THE FIGHTING GAMECOCK")

Perhaps no one epitomizes the indomitable fighting spirit of the South Carolina backcountry Patriot militia more than Thomas Sumter. Although a native of Virginia, Sumter led militia in several campaigns against local American Indian tribes and waged battles in the Revolutionary War before being wounded in 1780. Employing fierce guerilla-style tactics during raids on British camps, he was a constant thorn in the British side. Because the plucky Sumter was a known devotee of the grisly sport of cockfighting (illegal in all 50 states today), the British dubbed him the "Fighting Gamecock."

Sumter was such a hero in his adopted state of South Carolina that one town changed its name to Sumter and also adopted the general's fierce moniker by proclaiming itself the "Gamecock City." And, as many football fans know, the University of South Carolina team's nickname is the "Gamecocks." Sumter also was the name given to a certain island fort located in Charleston harbor. In 1861, the first shots of the Civil War were fired on Union soldiers garrisoned at Fort Sumter. Some 30 years prior to the beginning of that epic American struggle, however, Thomas Sumter passed away at the ripe old age of 97.

trail of 11.7 miles through the overarching, swampy netherworld, inhabited by alligators, bobcats, deer, and other critters.

NINETY SIX, MORE THAN JUST A NUMBER

Today we follow a northwesterly trajectory, leading deeper into South Carolina's Upcountry. We roll placidly over hillocks and then through a parade of exceptionally tall pine trees, which feel like narrow canyon walls. A sign declares the road to be a former Indian trail. Later, we cross over an impounded section of the Savannah River for a brief visit to Georgia.

In Elijah Clark State Park, we learn about one particular militia leader from Georgia. Elijah Clark organized and led backcountry fighters in various battles, including Musgrove's Mill, Cedar Springs, and more. A log cabin replica of the Clark home displays furniture, utensils and tools, dating to the 1780s.

Next, we arrive at the curiously named town of Ninety Six, SC, and Ninety Six National Historic

Site. We learn that Ninety Six, SC, is the modern-day version of the 18th-century preserved historic village of the same name. One possible explanation, among several, of how the colonial settlement acquired its numeric name involves English traders traveling the area in the 1700s. This site was estimated to be 96 miles from the Cherokee trading village of Keowee, near present-day Clemson.

During the Revolutionary War, Ninety Six was occupied and fortified by the British as a key strategic location for fighting the Patriots in South Carolina's backcountry. Continental Major General Nathaniel Greene and his force of around 1,000 Patriot troops laid siege to the settlement on May 22, 1781.

Strolling the grounds of the Ninety Six Historic Site, we better understand the tactics employed in 18th century warfare. Wooden towers, 30 feet high, gave sharpshooters a platform with clear lines of fire into Loyalist earthworks. Trenches also were dug progressively closer to the Loyalist Star Fort. Sapling

TIMELINE OF BRITAIN'S FAILED SOUTHERN STRATEGY

Date/Major Event

- **December 29, 1778**
  British capture Savannah, GA.
- **May 12, 1780**
  After a month-long siege, British capture the South's largest city and seaport, Charleston, SC (named Charles Town at that time).
- **May 29, 1780**
  Americans slaughtered, after raising the white flag, by British Colonel Tarleton's forces at the Battle of Waxhaws.
- **August 16, 1780**
  British defeat larger force of American Patriots at the Battle of Camden, SC.
- **October 7, 1780**
  Outnumbered Americans defeat British at the Battle of Kings Mountain, killing British commander Major Ferguson.
- **January 17, 1781**
  Patriot commander Daniel Morgan virtually destroys Tarleton's larger force at the Battle of Cowpens.
- **March 15, 1781**
  British defeat Americans at the Battle of Guilford Courthouse, but at a heavy cost, which forces British General Cornwallis to retreat to the North Carolina coast.
- **May 22 to June 19, 1781**
  American Southern commander Nathaniel Green lays siege to the important British outpost at Ninety Six.
- **October 19, 1781**
  British General Cornwallis surrenders to George Washington at Yorktown, VA.

tree branches were bound together into large cylindrical shapes, which attackers could roll toward the fort from a protected firing position behind them. Because 2,000 additional British troops were on the march to Ninety Six from Charleston, Greene had to withdraw from the siege on June 18. But, as the strains of backcountry battle escalated, the British eventually had to abandon Ninety Six.

UP AND INTO THE OTHER CAROLINA

The tranquil landscape at Musgrove Mill State Historic Site belies the savage fighting that took place here on August 19, 1780. Some 200 Patriot militiamen attacked what they believed was a comparable number of Loyalists. The Loyalist force, however, had been joined by 300 more fighters from the British post at Ninety Six. Nevertheless, the scrappy Overmountain Men from Tennessee gave the Loyalists an unforgettable, lopsided whooping.

A coiled snake of a route leads to our overnight accommodations in Brevard, NC. Climbing up into the Blue Ridge foothills on US 178, we enter into a succession of tight curves. The scenery is spectacular, but we don't take our eyes off the road for too long, because this narrow stretch of pavement requires our full, undivided attention.

Brevard has become a trendy art enclave and tourist destination. In the mountain coolness of the evening, Jeff and I walk the streets to select a dinner option from the many inviting eateries in the downtown area. We finally settle on Magpie Meat & Three. During our sumptuous repast, Jeff and I talk about the town's namesake, Ephraim Brevard. A Revolutionary War surgeon, Brevard was taken prisoner by the British and died in their custody.

TWO PIVOTAL SOUTHERN BATTLES

Our final day begins with another exhilarating trip down into South Carolina. We take US 276, a stretch of two-lane tarmac with tight curves and limited sight lines that achieves a crescendo of curves in Caesar's Head State Park. It's a nice route but can quickly punish the imprudent motorist. Once on SR 11, the curves are less intense. We navigate over gentle rolling hills and arrive at Cowpens National Battlefield. By 1781, the South had become the decisive theater of the Revolutionary War. Patriot General Daniel Morgan was commanding a combined force of Continentals and militia in this area when British General Cornwallis dispatched Banastre Tarleton to intercept them.

The visitor center and several audio tours detail the battle that helped turn the tide of war. Although outnumbered, Morgan halted his troops and prepared for battle on an open field primarily used for grazing cattle. He employed a counter offensive that utilized the superior shooting skills of his Patriot force and the longer effective range of their rifles. The brilliant double envelopment tactic worked to perfection, virtually decimating Tarleton's legion and sending him into a desperate retreat for his life.

Our final stop of the tour is at Kings Mountain National Military Park. This battle occurred in October 1780, four months prior to Cowpens. It showed the folly of Britain's Southern Strategy. Major Patrick Ferguson had staged his Loyalist troops atop a treeless, rocky spur of the Blue Ridge. Perched 150-forested-feet above the surrounding terrain, they awaited the Patriot force's arrival. Ferguson believed the high ground would be a superior tactical position.

The attacking Patriots encircled Kings Mountain and then maneuvered up it, dodging from tree to tree. The Loyalists were easy silhouette targets on the treeless summit. In a little over an hour of fighting, Ferguson was slain and his men were dead, wounded, or captured. This stunning loss wiped out British General Cornwallis' entire left flank. The Kings Mountain and Cowpens victories helped turn the tide of battle decisively in the Patriots' favor. Just nine

months later, Cornwallis had retreated to Yorktown, VA, and there surrendered to George Washington, effectively ending the war. On the trip home, I reflect on the rich history of South Carolina's Upcountry, where Patriots prevailed when America's future hung in the balance. Had the southern Patriots not been successful, we might be returning home today via a British vehicle. Just sayin.'

Monument commemorating Patriot General Daniel Morgan's victory over British forces at the Battle of Cowpens.

Always consult more-detailed maps for touring purposes. For map legend, see page 65.

FACTS & INFO

SOUTH CAROLINA REVOLUTIONARY TOUR

Approximately 900 miles

OVERVIEW

The mileage on this five-day tour is moderate so travelers have time to explore the battlefields and other points of interest. To avoid the crowds and summer heat and humidity, the best times to go are in the spring and fall. Accommodations and dining establishments ran the gamut from national chains to inviting family-owned businesses.

ROADS

Roads along the route are generally in very good condition and not heavily trafficked. US.178 and US 276, to and from North Carolina are very well suited for folks who like challenging curves in mountainous terrain.

RESOURCES

- **South Carolina Tourism**
  www.discoversouthcarolina.com
- The American Revolution in **South Carolina**
  www.carolana.com/SC/Revolution

POINTS OF INTEREST

1. **Historic Brattonsville, SC**
   www.chmuseums.org/brattonsville
2. **Andrew Jackson State Park, Lancaster SC**
   www.southcarolinaparks.com/andrewjackson
3. **Landsford Canal State Park, Catawba, SC**
   www.southcarolinaparks.com/landsfordcanal
4. **Congaree National Park, Hopkins, SC**
   www.nps.gov/cong
5. **Elijah Clark State Park, Lincolnton, GA**
   www.gastateparks.org/ElijahClark
6. **Ninety Six National Historic Site**
   Ninety Six, SC, www.nps.gov/nisi
7. **Cowpens National Battlefield, Gaffney, SC**
   www.nps.gov/cowp
8. **Kings Mountain National Military Park**
   Blacksburg, SC, www.nps.gov/kimo

Download the RoadRUNNER Rides app for turn-by-turn directions.

INDIAN REMOVAL IN THE 19TH CENTURY:

As Europeans continued flooding into America in the 19th century, our federal government began displacing Native Americans from their homelands by moving them to reservations west of the Mississippi River. This section retraces the paths followed by one of those tribes, the Cherokee, along what came to be known as The Trail of Tears, because of the resulting deaths and hardships.

THE CHEROKEE TRAIL OF TEARS

Missionary Daniel Butrick kept a journal of his travels with the Cherokee People as they were force-marched to Indian Territory during the winter of 1838-39. It is one of the saddest episodes in American history, with the depths of despair grippingly described by him in this entry: "… *the government might more mercifully have put to death everyone under a year or over sixty; rather it had chosen a more expensive and painful way of exterminating these poor people.*"

BREAKING AWAY FROM THE BELTWAY

In pre-Columbian times, the Cherokee People's land stretched from the Ohio River to present-day Kentucky, Tennessee, North Carolina, South Carolina, Georgia, and Alabama. But by the early 1800s, various treaties had reduced Cherokee land to a fraction of their former size. At the same time, European diseases devastated much of the Cherokee Nation. Those who survived adopted many aspects of Eu-

ropean culture and enterprise, including farming, a written language, a court system, a printed newspaper, and even Christianity. Cherokee settlements looked and functioned much the same as white settlements of the day. However, in 1828, gold was discovered on Cherokee land in North Georgia, and white settlers began ignoring legal Cherokee boundaries. By 1830, the Cherokee had lost any legal claim to their lands. That year, Congress passed the Indian Removal Act, and President Andrew Jackson signed it into law; he had long advocated Indian removal to lands west of the Mississippi River.

Bob Brown and I start our journey at the US Capitol in Washington, DC, on a hot, humid day in early September. After touring the National Museum of the American Indian, it's time to motor south and explore the Cherokee Trail of Tears. Bob (my intrepid travel companion on this long-distance adventure) and I spend the next three days enjoying the stunning scenery of the Blue Ridge Parkway on our way to Cherokee, NC.

INSUFFICIENTLY CELEBRATED GENIUS

Cherokee, NC, is the present-day home base for the Eastern Band of Cherokee Indians, descendants of some 800 who remained after the other 15,000 members of the tribe were forced to resettle in Indian Territory (present-day Oklahoma). Today, Cherokee, NC is a small but vibrant resort town. Gaming establishments are available for adults, and a host of outdoor activities and shopping venues abound. But Bob and I are focused on learning more about the Cherokee People themselves. There's no better place to start than the Museum of the Cherokee Indian in downtown Cherokee. We spend several hours perusing numerous artifacts, exhibits, sculptures, dioramas, and other artwork recounting Cherokee culture and seminal events in Cherokee history. It's easy to see why some referred to them as one of the "Five Civilized Tribes," virtually all of which were removed from the southeastern states. By late morning we're back on the pavement following some of the region's most iconic roads. My goal in designing this route was to enjoy interesting roads between the various Trail of Tears historical sites. First up is the Tail of the Dragon. Although it's a relatively short distance, the 318 curves make it seem much longer—it can be an exhausting experience to navigate.

DESTINATION:
MUSEUM OF THE CHEROKEE INDIAN

The museum's stated mission is "to perpetuate the history, culture, and stories of the Cherokee People." Cherokee artifacts show continual occupation in the southern Appalachian Mountains for more than 13,000 years. The Museum of the Cherokee Indian tells their story, dating from the Paleo, Archaic Woodland, and Mississippian periods through present-day. Approximately 800 to 1,000 Cherokee people stayed in this area, their original homeland, when most of the tribe was forcibly removed to Indian Territory (present-day Oklahoma) in 1838. This group is now known as the Eastern Band of Cherokee Indians. Today, they number approximately 13,000, with about 9,000 living on tribal land.

The "Emissaries of Peace: The 1762 Cherokee & British Delegations" exhibit focuses on when Cherokee leaders traveled to London to meet with King George III. Henry Timberlake, who accompanied the tribal leaders, kept a memoir, which the exhibit brings to life with artifacts, archaeological treasures, period artwork, music, and life-size figures. Because of the exhibit's excellence in telling this story, it has previously been on display at the National Museum of American History in Washington, DC.

I found the sculpture of a Cherokee man celebrating the Green Corn Festival to be particularly evocative. The figure's sculptor is Jerry Wolfe, who participated in the Normandy Beach landing on D-Day in World War II, was also a part-time tribal storyteller at the museum. He holds the esteemed title of Beloved Man of the Eastern Band of Cherokee Indians. (Sadly, Jerry passed away in 2018 at the age of 93.) Find it at 589 Tsali Blvd, Cherokee, NC, (828) 497-3481, www.cherokeemuseum.org.

Continuing farther west, to an island in Tennessee's Tellico Lake , we find reconstructed Fort Loudon. The British colony of South Carolina built the original fort here during the French and Indian War (1754-1763). This helped to ally the Overhill Cherokee Nation in the fight with the French and preserve trade with the Cherokee. But relations broke down in the 19th century, and the Cherokee captured Fort Loudon in August 1860.

A mile farther down the road we find the Sequoyah Birthplace Museum. Sequoyah (1776-1843) was a soldier, statesman, silversmith, blacksmith, and, most importantly, creator of the written Cherokee language. His development of the Cherokee sylla-bary marked one of the few times in history that a member of a preliterate people independently created an effective writing system. The Cherokee Nation officially adopted Sequoyah's syllabary, and their literacy rate soon surpassed that of surrounding European-American settlers.

We cap off our day of discovery with an exhilarating excursion back into North Carolina on the gloriously scenic Cherohala Skyway. The majestic, tree-lined mountains and stunning panoramas take our breath away as the road carves through the landscape.

RAINY ROADS TO ROME

Today, we'll test the theory that all roads do, in fact, lead to Rome—after all, our destination is Rome … Georgia. We begin our circuitous route with a leaden sky and a light fog, all harbingers of the day's weather conditions to come. State Routes 2 and 52, taking us west from historic Ellijay, GA, turn out to be really curvy. The narrow, two-lane tarmac writhes back and forth as we gain altitude. This might be fun except for one thing: Rain is coming down in torrents, diminishing visibility to several yards. We pull off at the visitor center in Fort Mountain State Park to wait out the deluge; better safe than sorry.

By the time we reach the Chief Vann House State Historic Site in Chatsworth, sunlight is filtering through high clouds. Construction of this two-and-a-half-story Colonial-style brick home was completed in 1804. James Vann established the largest and most prosperous plantation in the Cherokee Nation. His well-to-do life, however, was cut short in 1809—and eventually his family's holdings were later also lost when the Cherokee were forcibly removed from their homeland.

We travel to nearby Calhoun, which was once New Echota, GA, the capital of the Cherokee Nation and official starting point of the Trail of Tears. At the New Echota Historic Site, the original town layout has been re-plotted, and a number of buildings, including a council house, courthouse, print shop, residences, and general store, have been recon-structed. New reconstructions proceed as funds permit. All of the original buildings here were laid to waste, and the Cherokee lands redistributed to non-native settlers by lottery, once the Cherokee had been forced out.

In its day, New Echota represented the apex of Cherokee culture and government. But, unfortu-nately, Cherokee also committed acts of treachery against their fellow tribesmen here. A small mi-nority of unofficial representatives of the Cherokee Nation signed the Treaty of New Echota with the US government on December 29, 1835. The treaty ceded all Cherokee territory in the southeast and formed the legal basis for their removal to Indian Territory. This act set in motion the Trail of Tears and bitter resentments toward the illegitimate group of signers, known as the Treaty Party. As we arrive at our hotel in Rome, I recall that violent revenge would be exacted on the Treaty Party in years to come.

We motor west along rural country lanes into Northern Alabama. Prior to removal, this area was also part of the Cherokee Nation. Signage periodically confirms that our route follows the historic Trail of Tears. At this point, however, it's important to note that there was not a single trail, and the removal took place in two stages: the roundup and then the transport to Indian Territory. Soldiers arrived at Cherokee settlements and gave inhabitants little time to gather what few belongings they could carry. Then they marched them to makeshift holding forts, which offered little to no protection from the elements. Many died of exposure and diseases before ever starting the long trek to Indian Territory.

CHUGGING INTO CHATTANOOGA

The Trail of Tears transport phase actually occurred over several different routes, some of which involved conveyance by river for part of the distance and walking for the remainder. But most of the Cherokee walked or rode in wagons to their new homeland. The northern overland route, which is probably the most infamous, and the one most Cherokee followed, required them to walk around 1,200 miles with inadequate clothing, shelter, and food during one of the coldest winters on record.

Arriving in Fort Payne, AL, we turn north. There's little reminder here today that the original Fort Payne was constructed by the Alabama militia in 1838 as one of the many internment camps for holding Cherokee during the roundup phase of Indian removal. After departure of the last group on October 3, 1838, the fort was promptly abandoned.

In Trenton, GA, we head east, following the narrow, curvy road leading up Lookout Mountain. The steep asphalt ascent reaches a plateau at the Chickamauga Civil War Battlefield. Although Confederate forces won the battle here in September 1863, renewed fighting in Chattanooga in November gave Union forces a victory and control of the city. Chattanooga was known as the "Gateway to the Deep South." After the fighting a Confederate soldier ominously wrote, "This … is the death-knell of the Confederacy."

The entrance to Point Park is a double stone turret with a walkway through the structure's connecting arch. This iconic castle-themed edifice is also the symbol for the US Army's Corps of Engineers. At the brow of Lookout Mountain, we're treated to a stunning panoramic vista of Chattanooga and the Tennessee River far below.

Just down the road, in Rossville, GA, is the former home of John Ross, long-serving Principal Chief of the Cherokee Nation. He led the tribe's official government and its opposition to Cherokee removal. The two-story log structure became a National Historic Landmark in 1973. The fenced-off site currently has limited times and dates for visitor access. We follow the Lookout Mountain Scenic Highway down to the Tennessee River and into Chattanooga, TN. As we arrive at our overnight lodging at the historic Chattanooga Choo Choo Hotel, I spot a road sign confirming that we are still on the Trail of Tears. After the Cherokee roundup, Chattanooga became a main departure point for the long journey to Indian Territory.

The next morning, we go to Chattanooga's riverfront and find the historical sign for Ross's Landing, named, of course, after Principal Chief John Ross. On June 6, 1838, over 1,500 Cherokee departed from this point on steamboats and barges. The final group left here in the fall but had to begin their journey on foot due to low water levels.

Later in the day we arrive at Red Clay State Historic Area just north of the Georgia border. This location became the temporary Cherokee capital after Georgia forced them out of New Echota in 1832. The park has several reconstructed Cherokee village buildings, a visitor center, gift shop, and planned programs.

TRAVERSING TENNESSEE

After several warm days, we awake to lower humidity and temperatures in the low 50s. Cobalt blue skies greet us as we ease our way into traffic. It always feels invigorating to get back on the road, especially in such pleasant weather.

"Left Brainerd for the Cherokee camps … Thus we leave this place, perhaps never to return." —The Journal of Rev. Daniel S. Butrick, October 4, 1839.

Reverend Butrick departed from Calhoun, TN, with the Richard Taylor Detachment on the overland

Northern Route. Bob Brown, and I , however, initially follow a paved approximation of Bell's Route west from Ross's Landing in Chattanooga. Along the way to Oklahoma, we will travel segments of several Trail of Tears routes. Following the Tennessee River west, our route ascends part of the way up Lookout Mountain on switchbacks. Then, we descend and stay close to the river for a while, but tall trees largely obscure it from sight.

Finally, the river makes a sweeping bend south as we continue west. We're soon following a sinuous path and gaining altitude popping out on top of a

Washington D.C. to Tennessee

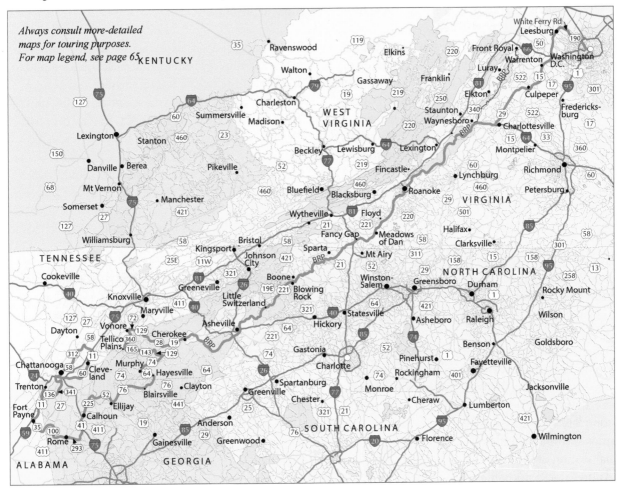

Always consult more-detailed maps for touring purposes. For map legend, see page 65

high ridge. Flatter terrain greets our descent into Cowan, TN. The town's vintage railroad depot, with a 1920 Porter steam locomotive and rolling stock parked outside, is now the Cowan Railroad Museum. A restored Texaco service station across the street adds to the town's mid-20th-century charm. But it's Sunday and most everything is closed. The

in Nashville, where Cherokee on the Northern Route passed through during their removal journey. At the pedestrian entrance, a vertical banner displays an image of Jackson gallantly riding a white horse with his saber drawn and raised high in the air. Above the image is a jagged lightning bolt and text declaring that our seventh president was

Cherokee mothers tearfully
offered their children to white settlers
so that they might survive.

Trail of Tears Interpretive Center in nearby Pulaski, TN, is a former Baptist church, which was relocated here. Pulaski is significant because it's where the Benge and Bell trails intersected on their two different routes to Indian Territory. John Benge departed from Fort Payne on September 28, 1838, escorting 1,079 Cherokee. John Bell, a member of the "Treaty Party," left Fort Cass on October 11, 1838, with 660 Cherokee. Outside of the center stands life-sized bronze statuary of a Cherokee family. It hauntingly depicts people uprooted from their homeland and forced to undergo the grueling journey west.

A MAN BORN FOR A STORM
Before leaving Lawrencebrug, TN, we stop at David Crockett State Park. One of its attractions is an original section of the Trail of Tears. But there's little here, besides a few historical signs, to commemorate the Cherokee pilgrimage; ol' Davey seems to be the main point of interest in his namesake park.

After continuing several more miles west, we head north on the Natchez Trace Parkway to join the northern route in Nashville. No journey along the Tennessee portion of the Trace, however, is complete without stopping to pay respects at the gravesite of Meriwether Lewis. There's also an original section of the Natchez Trace close by. Ironically, Andrew Jackson's home, The Hermitage, is located

"BORN FOR A STORM." Since Bob has never been to The Hermitage, we go in for a tour of the building and grounds.

The docents speak of Jackson's life at The Hermitage before, during, and after his presidency, and of his accomplishments as a military leader and as president. But there's virtually no mention of the Trail of Tears or the Indian Removal Act, despite him having signed it into law. Outside the entry turnstile, though, is a larger-than-life twenty dollar bill with an oval opening where Jackson's bust would normally appear. Tourists line up to have their picture taken as the currency's fresh face. Someone here must have a sense of humor, or at least a fuller sense of American history.

After a full day of fascinating sights and discoveries, we're relieved to arrive at our overnight accommodations in Clarksville, TN, not far from the Kentucky border.

ON TO THE OHIO
On December 3, 1838, Rev. Daniel Butrick wrote the following in his journal:

"We started in the morning. The ground was mostly covered in snow and frozen rain. We traveled about 12 miles, and camped within half a mile of Hopkinsville."

We cross the Kentucky border, and soon spot the Trail of Tears Commemorative Park entrance in Hopkinsville. It's situated on a portion of the former campground used by the Cherokee on their trek along the northern route. Two Cherokee chiefs, White Path and Fly Smith, died from illness contracted on the trail and are buried in the adjoining cemetery. Near the gravesites, full-scale sculptures powerfully convey the forlorn state of the Cherokee people, who suffered under the trail's many privations.

We pass by another documented Cherokee campsite, known as Big Spring, in Princeton, KY. Nearing the Ohio River, we stop at the Mantle Rock Preserve. A meandering dirt path leads us deep into the woods until we finally get to the geologic structure named Mantle Rock. This natural sandstone bridge spans 188 feet and rises to 30 feet overhead. It's reportedly the largest freestanding arch east of the Mississippi River. In the winter of 1838, more than 1,400 Cherokee spent two weeks in this area, waiting for the Ohio River to thaw so they could cross it.

After hiking back to the road, we continue on a short way to the Ohio River bank, where a historical marker denotes the former location of Berry's Ferry. Rev. Butrick noted in his journal, on December 15, 1838:

"Early in the morning the detachment started for the river, and commenced crossing about 10 o'clock. … As we were now passing out of a slave state into a free, we reflected on the pleasures of landing where all were in a measure free. But we had scarcely landed when we were met with volleys of oaths from every quarter."

The Cherokee, having had little to eat during the previous two weeks, were reportedly charged one dollar a head to cross the Ohio on Berry's Ferry. The normal rate was only twelve cents. Traversing the southern tip of Illinois, between the Ohio and

Mississippi Rivers, would prove to be one of the most difficult and heartbreaking sections of the northern route migration.

TRAPPED IN ILLINOIS

After overnighting on the outskirts of Metropolis, IL, we cruise through Superman's make-believe hometown, where there's lots of Man of Steel kitsch to draw in visitors. Making our way north on a rural road to rejoin the northern route, I spot a gentleman sitting in an old, straight-back wooden chair on his small farm. What's unusual about the scene is that his back is turned to the road. I surmise that he has arrived at a point in life when he is no longer curious about passersby and where they might be going. Instead, he seems to be looking at his home place and possibly reflecting on his life there in years past.

Once crossing the Ohio River, Rev. Butrick's party, and several others, could not continue; ice floes made ferrying across the Mississippi River impossible. On January 1, 1839, Rev. Butrick penned this entry in his journal:

"Thus we enter on a new year in this wilderness about 25 miles from the Mississippi. I say wilderness, because, though many people are settled around us, yet we, Indians, have a little spot of woodland assigned to us, in which we must reside as really as if all the region were a wilderness. White people come to sell and get gain, but not to invite any to a friendly roof."

I recall meeting a couple from Illinois on a stop along the Blue Ridge Parkway several days ago. The woman had grown up in southern Illinois. She related her family's oral history, which bore witness to the dire conditions the Cherokee faced while they were trapped between the Ohio and Mississippi Rivers. She said the winter was so severe in 1838-39 that many of the children died from disease, exposure, and malnutrition. Cherokee mothers tearfully offered their children to white settlers so that they might survive. She then told us that an ancestor of hers was one of them.

In the 21st century, our crossing of the Mississippi River is just a matter of coasting over a bridge to Cape Girardeau, MO. We keep going, though, several miles north to Trail of Tears State Park. This is where nine of the 13 Cherokee groups crossed the Mississippi by ferry, once it was finally free of ice. The park has a panoramic river overlook and a visitor center with exhibits that tell the Trail of Tears saga. We stay the night just east of Cape Girardeau and look forward to following the northern route into central Missouri tomorrow, where our path will intersect with a segment of Historic Route 66.

MIDWAY IN MISSOURI

The next day of our journey starts out cool enough, with temperatures only in the 60s. But, before we reach our destination, it will soar well into the 90s. The topography in eastern Missouri is steep and hilly. We seem to be constantly climbing or descending, with frequent blind curves sprinkled in along the way.

An enthusiastic pace causes me to pass the Snelson-Brinker Cabin in a flash, but we negotiate a quick U-turn and park in the small gravel lot. The cabin, owned by John Brinker in the late 1830s, was constructed in 1834. Several detachments of Cherokee traveling the northern route camped on the property. Tragedy struck, however, when four members of the Richard Taylor Detachment died while camped here. They are buried on the property in the family cemetery. This was unusual at the time, because many white cemeteries didn't allow Indian burials.

Just down the road is Meramec Spring Park. With an average of 100 million gallons of water flowing through the spring daily, this was a hospitable camping location for Cherokee on the northern route. Signs denote trail segments in the park; several museums house cultural and historical exhibits. Our day ends in St. Robert, MO, which is about halfway on our journey from Chattanooga to the western Cherokee capital in Tahlequah, OK.

OZARK BYWAYS

The next morning, we continue our journey along the Cherokee Trail of Tears from St. Robert (near Waynesville) in central Missouri.

"We travelled about 12 miles to a settlement called Port Royal (believed to be Waynesville by researchers), on the banks of a beautiful stream, named Rubedoo. Here we had a delightful place, on the bank of the river, convenient to wood and water. We employed our kind Nancy, a black woman to wash, and dried our clothes in the evening by the fire."
—Rev. Daniel Butrick, March 12, 1839

We soon arrive at Missouri's historic Roubidoux Spring. The encampment history at this location, below a bluff in today's Laughlin Park, is told via an interpretive tour. Roubidoux Spring, with a daily flow of 37 million gallons of water, made this one of the better locations for Cherokee encampment. The spring was named after French trapper Joseph Roubidoux. Today, fly fishermen are submerged up to their waists in the cold water trying to hook a brown or rainbow trout. The spring is also a favorite location for another activity that the migrating Cherokee would have found quite incomprehensible: scuba cave diving! At the cave entrance, I peer down through clear rushing water into the black-as-coal opening into a subterranean water world. The northern route of the Trail of Tears continued southwest from here to Springfield, MO, before turning south into Arkansas.

Diving deeper into the Ozarks' rural two-lane roads, we travel back in time at another popular fishin' hole in Rockbridge, MO. Ice-cold Spring Creek cascades over the dam at historic Rockbridge Mill. This former mill town is now the Rainbow Trout & Game Ranch, which attracts sportsmen and women from far and wide. At the combination post office and restaurant, we enjoy a sumptuous meal of—what else? Freshly caught rainbow trout.

The final leg of today's journey takes us across the Arkansas border to a lake that I have fond memories of scuba diving in. Scuba diving may not be for me now, but I was young the last time I was here. Our overnight lodging is situated on a hill overlooking Norfork Lake. From the small deck of my cabin, I watch the setting sun suffuse sky and water in a warm glow.

CLINTON COUNTRY

One of my favorites in this part of Arkansas is Push Mountain Road, which winds its way across several high ridges with breathtaking vistas. Continuing

south, we pass through quaint Ozark towns, but the scenery turns to 21st-century suburbia as we draw nearer to Little Rock. We stop to check out the William J. Clinton Presidential Center. The modernist-styled building is positioned dramatically on the banks of the Arkansas River. Inside there's a replica of Clinton's Oval Office, where, for a small fee, one can have their picture taken while sitting at the former president's desk.

I would like to say that we resisted this touristy invitation, but we didn't. Outside, a former railroad bridge over the Arkansas River has been converted to a pedestrian walkway. We linger there for a while, watching a tugboat slowly push barges upriver.

THE WATER ROUTE

Next morning, we roll west following the Arkansas River. Several of the Trail of Tears routes passed through or near Little Rock. Cherokee traveling on the water route from Tennessee were on the

Tennessee to Missouri

DESTINATION: WOOLAROC MUSEUM & WILDLIFE PRESERVE

This former ranch, set in northeastern Oklahoma's rolling Osage Hills, was built in 1925 by Frank Phillips, founder of Phillips Petroleum, as his weekend and holiday sanctuary. The rustic grounds have an assortment of fauna, including buffalo, elk, zebra, water buffalo, deer, elk, Longhorn cattle, and more. Just so visitors won't be confused about the source of funding for Woolaroc, one of Phillips iconic cottage-style gas stations is located on the entrance road.

The property's historic lodge home is now the Woolaroc Museum, which has one of the finest collections of Southwest art in the world. The galleries feature paintings and sculptures by many legendary Indian and Western artists in American history: Frederic Remington, Charles M. Russell, William R. Leigh, Thomas Moran, Frank Tenney Johnson, and others. Frank Phillips acquired much of the collection during his lifetime, especially pieces produced by the more classical artists. In later years the collection has been enhanced by donations from Phillips family members.

But it's one particular piece of Native American art that made the Woolaroc Museum my chosen terminus. Robert Lindneux was an American Western artist who captured many important transformations in history. The evocative image of suffering endured by the Cherokee people during their forced removal was brilliantly captured in Lindneux's 1942 painting Trail of Tears. Studying Oklahoma history as a youngster in the former Indian Territory, I often saw this haunting image displayed in textbooks and other materials. And now I'm standing before the actual painting. It's magnificent! Find it at 1925 Woolaroc Ranch Rd, Bartlesville, OK, (918) 336-0307, www.woolaroc.org.

Arkansas River, while others went overland just north of it.

The first of three Arkansas River overlooks is at Pinnacle Mountain State Park. A historical sign, titled "They Passed This Way," tells the story of Indians traveling on the removal boats along this section of the Water Route. A song, reportedly heard on several boats, had these lyrics:

"I have no more land. I am driven away from home, driven up the red waters, let us all go, let us all die together and somewhere upon the banks we will be there."

On the brow of a bluff in Petit Jean State Park, our eyes are treated to a panoramic vista of the Arkansas River meandering below, a verdant agricultural landscape in the river valley, and smoky silhouettes of the Ozark Mountains are in the far distance. We break for lunch at Mather Lodge and enjoy the food and more breathtaking mountain scenery through the restaurant's windows.

After lunch we take a tight, winding road to the summit of Mt. Nebo, where more breathtaking views of the Arkansas River Valley await. Unlike the Cherokee traveling the river on rafts, we have a beautiful day to appreciate nature's splendor. After descending, we follow U.S. 64, which is a designated Trail of Tears overland route, to overnight lodging in Clarksville, AR.

Heading north from Clarksville, we end up on several of Arkansas's most notable curvy roads: State Roads 21, 16, 45, and 303 all put big smiles on our faces. We take a breather at historic War Eagle Mill, which is perched picturesquely on the banks of War Eagle Creek. We cross over the creek on an antique steel trellis bridge (circa 1907) with a wooden plank surface.

Continuing north we soon reach Pea Ridge National Military Park, but it's not Civil War history that brings us here. The original Elkhorn Tavern was located in this spot on a stretch of Telegraph Road,

which was also part of the northern route. The Richard Taylor contingent of Cherokees reportedly camped here in March of 1839. After the original tavern was burned during the Civil War, it was reconstructed in 1865.

Many people from the so-called Five Civilized Tribes, who were displaced by the Indian Removal Act, passed through Arkansas on their way to assigned lands in Indian Territory. It's hard to go very

Missouri to Oklahoma

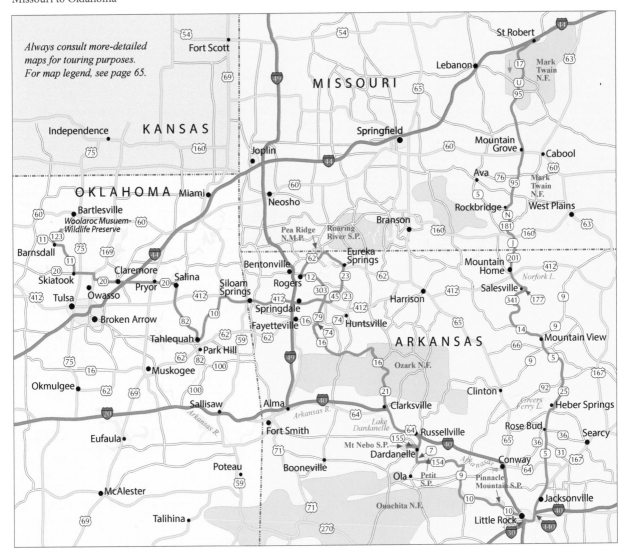

far in western Arkansas without crossing a marked or unmarked removal route.

Traveling to historic Eureka Springs, AR, we navigate through an area of the Ozarks known as the Boston Mountains. This landscape has more of an alpine feel to it; the serpentine roads are delightful and scenic. We celebrate in the evening with a superb meal at the 1886 Crescent Hotel & Spa.

going. But in life all good things, inevitably, must come to an end.

We get to Tahlequah, OK, the Western Cherokee capital, by late morning. After arriving here in 1839, the surviving Cherokee began rebuilding their lives, culture, and tribal economy. The tribal government buildings were initially log and frame structures, but were destroyed during the Civil War, a conflict that

The Cherokee have not only survived heart wrenching adversity, but are prospering in the 21st century.

END OF THE TRAIL

Sunday, March 31, 1839, was the final day of the Taylor detachment's grueling passage to Indian Territory. As recorded in Reverend Butrick's journal, with noticeable bitterness, it was not a particularly happy day:

"Mr. Taylor told me that the officers from Fort Gibson had sent word that they should be here today to take the detachment off his hands, and therefore should not be able to attend the meeting (worship service). Thus by means of the U. States officers the first Sabbath in the country must be profaned by almost every individual in the detachment. We had a meeting, however, and a considerable number of our Cherokee brethren attended. I endeavored to warn them of the dangers & temptations that await them."

Fast forward to the 21st century. This is our final day on the Trail of Tears. After several weeks of a regimented travel schedule, I'm looking forward to several days of rest. On the other hand, the prospect of tomorrow not traveling cross-country on some off-the-grid, two-lane byway is a little sad. Having been in a daily routine of seeing new places, meeting new people, and being constantly on the move, I often think I would just like to keep

bitterly divided members of the tribe. The Cherokee Supreme Court Building, built in 1844, is still standing in downtown Tahlequah. This structure, which is reportedly the oldest public building in Oklahoma, is now a museum. The Cherokee Nation Judicial Branch is housed in the former Cherokee Capitol Building, which was first occupied in 1870.

Once settled in Indian Territory, the Cherokee continued their industrious ways. Today, the Cherokee Nation's business interests include gaming, construction, aerospace and defense, manufacturing, technology, real estate, and healthcare. The Nation's estimated economic contribution to the State of Oklahoma is in excess of $1 billion annually.

There is one more destination to visit: Woolaroc Museum, near Muskogee, OK. Robert Lindneux's painting, Trail of Tears, is part of an impressive Western art collection assembled by Phillips Petroleum founder Frank Phillips. We'll travel the remaining miles there tomorrow and then our long journey of discovery will be complete. While this epic journey has been about a ghastly chapter in 19th century American history, we're pleased to see that the Cherokee have not only survived the heart wrenching adversity, but are prospering in the 21st century.

FACTS & INFO
CHEROKEE TRAIL OF TEARS

Download the RoadRUNNER Rides
app for turn-by-turn directions.

Approximately 2,910 miles

OVERVIEW

This tour dives deep into Native American history. The route winds its way south from Washington, DC, through some of the most scenic countryside on the East Coast. The "roundup" phase of Indian removal forcibly transfers Cherokee People from their homes and places them in crude holding forts in southeastern states to await their transfer to departure sites. In the transport phase Cherokee are moved from their holding pens to departure locations for the trip to Indian Territory. There are four main routes involving overland and water transport. We mostly follow the overland route to the former Indian Territory (modern day Oklahoma). Fall is the best time to make the trip, when the weather is milder and the risk of severe storms is lower.

ROADS

As mentioned previously, one of the goals of this tour was to link Trail of Tears historical sites with scenic roads to travel. Our favorite roads included: Blue Ridge Parkway, Hell Bender 28, Tail of the Dragon, Cherohala Skyway, Natchez Trace Parkway, SR 156, and US 41A in Tennessee, and surviving sections of Historic Route 66 in Central Missouri, Push Mountain Road and State Routes 16, 21, and 155 in Arkansas, and Scenic Route 10 in Oklahoma. Pavement is in good to very good condition.

POINTS OF INTEREST

- **National Museum of the American Indian**
  Washington, DC, www.nmai.si.edu
- **Fort Loudon State Historic Area, Vonore, TN**
  www.fortloudoun.com
- **Sequoyah Birthplace Museum, Vonore, TN**
  www.sequoyahmuseum.org
- **Chief Vann House**
  www.gastateparks.org/ChiefVannHouse
- **New Echota Historic Site, Calhoun, GA**
  www.gastateparks.org/NewEchota
- **John Ross House, Rossville, GA**
  www.tinyurl.com/john-ross
- **Point Park at Lookout Mountain**
  www.tinyurl.com/point-park
- **Ross's Landing, Chattanooga, TN**
- **Red Clay State Historic Park, Cleveland, TN**
- **Pulaski Trail of Tears Interpretive Center**
  www.nativehistoryassociation.org
- **Andrew Jackson's Hermitage**
  www.thehermitage.com
- **Trail of Tears Commemorative Park**
  Hopkinsville, KY, www.trailoftears.org
- **Berry's Ferry Site**, www.tinyurl.com/berrys-ferry
- **Trail of Tears State Park**, www.mostateparks.com
- **Maramec Spring Park-Massey Iron Works**
  www.maramecspringpark.com
- **Roubidoux Spring, Waynesville, MO**
  www.visitpulaskicounty.org/roubidoux.asp
- **Rockbridge Mill, Rockbridge, MO**
  www.rockbridgemo.com
- **Pinnacle Mountain State Park, Little Rock, AR**
  www.arkansasstateparks.com/pinnaclemountain
- **Petit Jean State Park, Morrilton, AR**
  www.petitjeanstatepark.com
- **War Eagle Mill, Rogers, AR**
  www.wareaglemill.com
- **Elkhorn Tavern, Pea Ridge, AR**
  www.scenicusa.net/021813.html
- **Cherokee Heritage Center, Park Hill, OK**
  www.cherokeeheritage.org
- **George M. Murrell Home, Park Hill, OK**
  www.okhistory.org/sites/georgemurrell.php

INDUSTRIALIZING AMERICA:

The 18th and 19th centuries were a time when America was boldly industrializing its manufacturing and transportation processes. The following two articles are about how mass production took root in New England and how the manual excavation of canals in New York helped transform it into the Empire State.

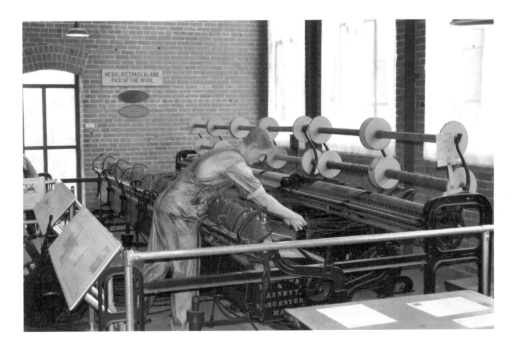

AMERICAN INDUSTRIAL REVOLUTION
CONNECTICUT, RHODE ISLAND, MASSACHUSETTS, NEW HAMPSHIRE, AND VERMONT

When British immigrant Samuel Slater introduced the first mechanized system of spinning cotton in the 1790s, America was still an agrarian society with a widely dispersed population, but that would soon start changing.

Jeff Arpin and I have reconnected for another road adventure into American history. We have traveled to Connecticut to begin exploring our nation's industrial heritage. Jeff also will be tracing his ancestral connection to America's Industrial Revolution.

WHERE THE REVOLUTION BEGAN
"Every revolution was first a thought in one man's mind, and when the same thought occurs to another man, it is the key to that era." – Ralph Waldo Emerson

A crisp, sunlit fall morning greets our departure from Willimantic, CT, home of the iconic Frog Bridge. On each of the 475-foot bridge's four corners is a giant frog sculpture sitting atop an oversized spool of thread. While the latter has a clear connection to the town's textile industrial history, the monuments' frog connection reads more like a fable. The legendary Battle of the Frogs reportedly occurred here in 1754. Startled town folk were awakened by the cacophonous shrieking of two opposing armies of small green amphibians in mortal combat. Apparently, it was about contested pond territory. Really?

We motor northeast into Connecticut's Quiet Corner where tree-shaded, two-lane byways are the norm. After strolling the River Mills Heritage Trail in Putnam, CT, we continue east into Rhode Island. Samuel Slater arrived in Pawtucket, RI, in 1789 with the thought of establishing a water-powered mill that could spin cotton into thread, something that he already had experience doing in his native England. When Slater Mill opened in 1793, it marked the beginning of a new era, which later became known as the American Industrial Revolution.

Slater Mill, in the 21st century, is a museum campus, which brings the American Industrial Revolution to life. The buildings are meticulously restored and, along with docents and signage, they illustrate how rushing water was converted into motive power by water wheels. These (in turn) drove gears, drive shafts, and large leather belts, which ultimately powered individual cotton-spinning machines. In an age where we take the manufacture of consumer products mostly for granted, the ingenuity of these nascent industrialists is fascinating.

THE FRENCH CONNECTION

Following the Blackstone River upstream, we stop in Woonsocket, RI, at the Museum of Work & Culture. Because it's Jeff's first visit to the town where his mother was born and raised, this is an especially poignant stop for him. Family farms in Quebec

DESTINATION:
LOWELL NATIONAL HISTORICAL PARK

Lowell, MA, was founded by Boston merchants in 1821 to 1822 as a purposely built factory city. It was sited on the Merrimack River to harness the water power produced by Pawtucket Falls, where the river plunges 32 feet in just one mile. Lowell and other industrial towns transformed America into a nation of urban manufacturing centers. Lowell, in many ways, was the epicenter of the American Industrial Revolution. Henry David Thoreau called Lowell the "Manchester of America, which sends its cotton cloth around the globe."

Lowell National Historical Park preserves and interprets for modern-day visitors a considerable swath of this 19th century manufacturing behemoth. Start at the Visitor Center for an overview of the power canal system, machines, workers, and entrepreneurs that propelled Lowell into a burgeoning industrial city. Next, take one of the replica open-car free trolleys on a two-mile trip to the Boott Mills stop for a tour of the restored mill house. Next door, in Boarding House Park, visitors can see the accommodations provided for the "mill girls"—those women who made up about two-thirds of Lowell's workforce.

The Lowell canal system siphoned water from the Merrimack River and distributed it throughout the city's expansive assortment of mills. The canals have been largely preserved and can be toured in ranger-guided canal boats. Other fascinating points of interest include the Suffolk Mills Turbine Exhibit, Pawtucket Gatehouse, Swamp Locks, and the Francis Gate & Guard Locks. Find it at 67 Kirk St, Lowell, MA, (978) 970-5000, www.nps.gov/lowe.

had become economically unsustainable, so Jeff's French-Canadian ancestors, along with thousands of their countrymen and women, began migrating to the Blackstone River Valley in the mid-19th century. Museum exhibits depict life working in the mills and the cultural life of Woonsocket. Because some 80 percent of the town residents were French speakers, both French and English were taught in public schools. Jeff notes that his grandfather worked in the mills as a child. Women and children were the labor force preferred by mill owners because they

Nevertheless, we're brimming with anticipation and curiosity about the day's main attraction, Lowell National Historical Park. Lowell, MA, was one of the most prolific mill towns during the American Industrial Revolution. This historical park is the largest site on our itinerary. The Boott Cotton Mills Museum has operating looms and interactive exhibits that demonstrate the manufacturing processes employed here. In an elongated room full of almost 100 looms, only four or five are active today, but the noise level is so high that it's uncomfortable

A docent tells us that when some 40,000 looms were running, back in Lowell's heyday, the noise could be heard from three miles away—most mill workers went deaf!

could be paid less than men. Children often performed maintenance in tight spaces of mill machinery. The typical work schedule was from 6 a.m. to 6 p.m., six days a week. With no ventilation inside the mills, it was stiflingly hot in the summer months and cold in the winter.

We head north toward our overnight destination in Worcester, MA, which was also a major location for contributions to the American Industrial Revolution. Industrial and consumer products, such as barbed wire, the monkey wrench, textile power looms, corsets, pottery, and more were manufactured in Worcester.

WHAT DID 40,000 LOOMS SOUND LIKE?
Shards of lightning dance outside the hotel windows as a weather front moves through during the nighttime hours. Morning dawns overcast with light rain, and the mercury registers 64 degrees. Because we're still within commuting range of Boston, secondary roads are congested with traffic. Potholes and rough pavement show the unmistakable toll of harsh winters.

to our ears. A docent tells us that when some 40,000 looms were running, back in Lowell's heyday, the noise could be heard from three miles away—most mill workers went deaf!

After sampling a few more exhibits and grabbing a quick lunch, we depart in a light rain. The Merrimack River leads north into New Hampshire and our overnight destination in Manchester.

LACONIA KNOCKS OUR SOCKS OFF
We start the morning off with cobalt blue skies and moderate temperatures, while enjoying New England's fall aromas. North of Manchester, NH, we finally escape the suburban reach of Boston and can fully appreciate these serene country byways. We ease up, though, in Laconia, NH. This historic town is located on the Winnipesaukee River, which powered mills between here and Lowell, MA.

Built in 1823, the Belknap Mill was later converted from weaving cloth to become one of America's first knitting factories and made socks for Union soldiers during the Civil War. Guides provide live

Water canal for powering weaving looms at the Lowell National Historical Park in Lowell, MA.

demonstrations of sock making on Thursdays. Besides preserving industrial artifacts and history, the museum's grounds also function as a town green by hosting cultural and other events (including a wedding on the Saturday of our visit).

Lake Winnipesaukee, only a few miles north, provides scenic panoramas as we travel along its southern shore. Rural two-lane tarmac then leads northeast across a rustic slice of New Hampshire's landscape. We finally stop at the base of the White Mountains in North Conway, NH. We're staying at a charming bed and breakfast that is just across the

road from the equally delightful Conway Scenic Railroad Station.

TOOLS OF PRECISION

After breakfast at the cozily informal Stairway Café, we ramble west on the famous Kancamagus Highway. The road's sinuous path cuts through White Mountain National Forest. The forest's natural beauty, in the form of mountain overlooks, rushing rivers, and waterfalls, is on abundant display.

Once we cross the Connecticut River, we find ourselves in Vermont where US 5 leads south to the American Precision Museum in Windsor, VT. It's housed in the former Robbins & Lawrence Armory and is believed to have the most historically significant collection of antique machine tools in America. Machine tools are important because they make possible the mass production of standardized interchangeable parts. For example, before the development of machine tools, muskets were handmade with no two being exactly the same.

MAKING MONEY BY MAKING MONEY

We make our way to the Crane Museum of Papermaking, located in Crane & Co.'s historic Old Stone Mill. The mill was built in 1844 on the banks of the Housatonic River. A small-scale demonstration of papermaking is in full swing just outside the front door. Inside, the history of American papermaking is on display in wall and floor cases.

Dating from Revolutionary War times, Crane & Co.'s durable cotton and linen papers have been used for currency, bond and stock certificates, as well as social and business correspondence. For seven generations, the Crane family business has reportedly been the sole supplier of currency paper for the U.S. Treasury.

It's nearing dusk when we arrive in Stockbridge, MA, for our overnight accommodations at the historic Red Lion Inn. Both the town and the inn are high among my favorite destinations in all of New England. After settling in our rooms, we savor a sumptuous repast in the inn's beautifully appointed main dining room.

including a functioning miniature steam-powered railroad. Today, the estate is fastidiously preserved by Connecticut as a state park. A docent leads us on a maze-like tour of the castle's interior. The secret passages and ornately hand carved wooden door

Designed by Gillette himself, the steel-supported stone structure of Gillette Castle required a team of 20 men five years to complete.

A CASTLE LIKE NO OTHER

It's getting progressively colder each morning; fall is definitely in the air. We find a warm window table at Stockbridge Coffee & Tea and enjoy a steaming hot breakfast. Town folk walk by with their collars turned up. They move briskly along the sidewalk; winter can't be too far away.

It's a sunny slog south on sweeping backroads. We stop in the picturesque town square of Westfield, MA, for hot soup and coffee. When we depart, we're met with almost blindingly bright September sunshine. A series of Connecticut byways and freeways finally lands us on the Connecticut River's western shore to wait for the ferry. A fanciful, dreamlike structure is perched proudly on the river's eastern bank—Gillette Castle.

William Gillette, a successful actor, director, and playwright built his 184-acre estate, called "Seventh Sister," here in 1914. The name derives from the castle's location on the southernmost hill in a chain known as the Seven Sisters. The centerpiece of the estate is the 24-room mansion, which resembles a surreal medieval castle.

Designed by Gillette himself, the steel-supported stone structure required a team of 20 men five years to complete. After his semi-retirement from the stage, Gillette directed the estate's many refinements,

latches contribute to the structure's whimsical ambiance. Gillette Castle proves to be a fitting conclusion to our tour of 19th century New England.

REFLECTION

In the digital age of the 21st century, physical artifacts from America's Industrial Revolution are rapidly disappearing; many of the old machines and buildings have been demolished or converted to other uses.

While bits and bytes can only be envisioned conceptually, the giant machinery of the industrial age appears unsophisticated (by today's standards) but ingenious in design and application. Visitors can readily visualize how these now quaint processes harnessed the power of nature to mass produce goods and put America on a path to extraordinary industrial might.

54

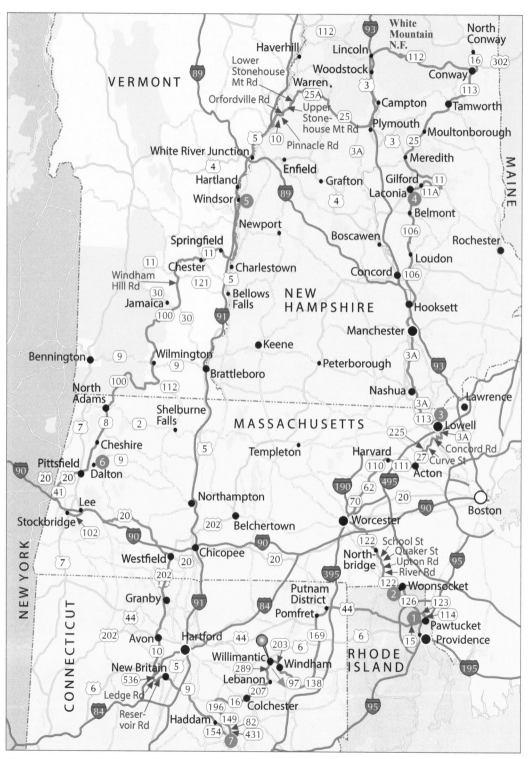

Always consult more-detailed maps for touring purposes. For map legend, see page 65.

FACTS & INFO

AMERICAN INDUSTRIAL REVOLUTION TOUR

Approximately 730 miles

OVERVIEW

Although this route can be taken anytime from spring through fall, the best time to go is in the fall when temperatures are moderate and the foliage is stunning. To allow time for perusing museums, daily mileage has been kept low. Several of the museums have been surrounded by urban sprawl and require riding in a few traffic-congested areas.

ROADS

New England scenery is often classic 19th century Americana, but because of severe winters, so are many of the road surfaces; frost heaves and potholes are abundant. Urban areas in central Connecticut, Rhode Island, eastern Massachusetts, and southern New Hampshire are heavily trafficked, but traffic is much scarcer in northern and western New England.

POINTS OF INTEREST

1. **Old Slater Mill, Pawtucket, RI**
   www.slatermill.org
2. **Museum of Work and Culture**
   Woonsocket, RI
   www.tinyurl.com/work-culture
3. **Lowell National Historic Park, Lowell, MA**
   www.nps.gov/lowe
4. **Belknap Mill, Laconia, NH**
   www.belknapmill.org
5. **American Precision Museum**
   Windsor, VT, www.americanprecision.org
6. **Crane Museum of Papermaking**
   Dalton, MA, www.cranemuseum.org
7. **Gillette Castle State Park, East Haddam, CT**
   www.ct.gov/deep/gillettecastle

 Download the RoadRUNNER Rides app for turn-by-turn directions.

NEW YORK WATERWAYS

In 1808, while still mayor of New York City, DeWitt Clinton began championing a grand vision: a system of canals providing the first all-water commercial shipping link from western New York and the Great Lakes to New York City, and from there to the rest of the world. At the time, many considered "Clinton's Ditch" to be a huge folly. Even President Thomas Jefferson, a fount of great visions himself, considered the idea of a 340-mile long, hand-dug canal from Albany to Buffalo to be "just short of madness." Nevertheless, in 1817, Clinton, now governor of New York, convinced the legislature to begin funding construction of the Erie Canal.

Still, given all of the negative press and sentiments of the times, the project took form and one of the greatest engineering marvels of its day, the Erie Canal was completed in 1825, after eight years of incredibly torturous labor. The construction of other New York canals soon followed and within a few years, by 1840, New York City had surpassed Philadelphia as the nation's chief seaport. New York was well on its way to becoming the "Empire State." And though most canals in America have long since vanished from the landscape, the New York Canal System lives on, enduring into the 21st century as a powerful magnet for tourism and recreation.

TO TICONDEROGA

After months of planning, Bruce Read (a friend and fellow traveling history buff) and I leave the Eisenhower Locks in Massena, NY. We navigate our way to US 11 east, following the general route of the historic Military Trail. Countries vying for control of the New World used many of the upstate New York waterways to conduct their military campaigns, and the relatively flat terrain between Massena, on the St. Lawrence River, and Lake Champlain provided

Reconstructed Fort Ticonderoga's armament pointed at a critical choke point, Lake Champlain, as it was during the War of 1812.

the shortest overland route for armies portaging from one waterway to another.

Near the Canadian border, the Adirondack Mountains rise majestically to our south, but a line of ominous-looking clouds trailing us eastward induces a slight alteration to our intended route, once we arrive on the shore of Lake Champlain at Rouses Point, NY. Rather than immediately taking the route of the Lakes to Locks Passage south to Plattsburgh, NY, we cross over an arm of Lake Champlain on US 2 and follow it south onto Grand Isle, Vermont. The lake is visible on our right and left and mountains dramatically frame both sides of Champlain Valley.

At the Grand Isle Ferry, we board with several other vehicles. During the 15-minute crossing to Plattsburgh, NY, my eyes scan the placid waters for any hint of the mythical sea monster "Champ," reputed to dwell within this deep glacial lake. The legend of this large horned serpent, or giant snake, stretches back to legends from indigenous native peoples, who hunted along the lake's shores. We arrive safe and sound in Plattsburgh, though, without any sign of Champy.

Reuniting with the Lakes to Locks Passage, we are surrounded by a bucolic landscape, and several miles south of Keeseville the Lakes to Locks Passage directs us onto SR 22. We follow the eastern base of the Adirondack Mountains on sinuous tarmac that is both less traveled and exceptionally scenic—always an excellent combination.

Twelve miles south of Plattsburgh, NY, a bridge carries us several hundred feet above what some call the Little Grand Canyon of the East. It's Ausable Chasm, which is about two miles long, ranging from 100 to 200 feet deep, and carved out over eons by the raging torrents of the Ausable River. Rainbow Falls, the highest of three waterfalls in the chasm, plunges 75 feet, creating a billowing cloud of mist in the afternoon sun. After parking, we peer over the bridge railing at the boiling cauldron of water slicing through sheer cliffs of Potsdam Sandstone. No wonder people come here from all over the world to see this stunning work of nature.

Farther south to Ticonderoga, NY, we're overtaken by those rain showers spotted earlier. The rain's intensity is a literal deluge, coming down so heavy that our vision of the road ahead is substantially reduced. We slow down, but finally arrive at our modest, but dry, accommodations.

TO WATERFORD
After a hearty breakfast at The Hot Biscuit Diner, we follow the only road up Mount Defiance. With expansive views of the Champlain Valley, the strategic importance of Fort Ticonderoga during the Revolutionary War is readily apparent from the mountain. Sited on a peninsula jutting out into a narrow, navigational choke point in the lake, the fort's cannons could easily inflict severe damage on any warships intent on maneuvering south of this point. But, there was just this one little problem with the fort's location. It was too close to the higher ground of Mount Defiance, and when British troops

managed to place two cannons there, they forced the American troops to surrender Fort Ticonderoga without firing a shot.

Inside, the fort's exhibits relate its colorful military history and the story of its ongoing restoration; while outside, a group of Fife and Drum Corps reenactors are providing the music to accompany a series of cannon-firing demonstrations. A series of special events are scheduled at the fort throughout the year.

Anxious to get back on the road, we continue on the Lakes to Locks Passage. Along the western shore of Lake Champlain, the lake narrows as we travel south. And at the picturesque village of Whitehall, NY, where the lake ends, the Champlain Canal

on The National Register of Historic Places and is open to visitors. Although Captain Skene was never a resident, the home's name was changed to Skene Manor by a subsequent owner in the 20th century. South along the Champlain Canal on US 4, there are many attractive towns that seem to have changed little over the years, retaining names like Fort Ann and Fort Edward which link our times to the struggles that gave birth to the Nation.

Late in the afternoon, we arrive in Waterford, NY, just north of Albany, where the waters of the Champlain Canal, the Hudson River, and the Erie Canal meet. Touring the visitor center, we meet the harbormaster, James Faraldi, who says that pleasure boats from as far away as Florida come here in the summer

The intriguing "sloped" lift bridge over the Erie Canal is listed in Ripley's Believe It or Not.

begins its 60-mile route to the Hudson River. Whitehall, along with several other locations on the Eastern Seaboard, lays claim to being the birthplace of the US Navy. Principally recognized at the time as a brilliant and daring Revolutionary War general, Benedict Arnold, oversaw construction of gunboats here and commanded the fleet that stalled the British advance on Saratoga, NY, in 1776. His notorious act of treason, at West Point, came later.

On this warm, humid day several pleasure boats rock gently at their moorings on the Champlain Canal in Whitehall, NY. The town was originally named Skenesborough, in 1765, after British Army Captain Philip Skene, but the name was changed to Whitehall after the American Revolutionary War. Skene Manor stands on a hill overlooking the harbor. Built in 1875, Skene Manor is a restored Victorian Gothic-style mansion, which is listed

months to cruise the New York Canal System. After an enjoyable dinner, I fall asleep thinking about the next day's journey along the famous Erie Canal, a waterway I have read and dreamed about since boyhood.

THE ERIE CANAL
We head off to follow the Erie Canal for the next two days. The first section of the waterway utilizes the Mohawk River, a tributary that flows east into the 315-mile Hudson River.

Since the original Erie Canal was completed in 1825, it was widened and dredged deeper in 1862, and then substantially enlarged and rerouted in 1918 to take greater advantage of existing rivers and lakes. The rerouting allowed a reduction in the number of locks from 83 to 35, substantially shortening the travel time along the 340-mile waterway. The Erie Canal spawned dramatic economic growth in western New York during the second half of the 19th century and the first half of the 20th century. However, by the late 1950s, commercial rail and truck transportation offered shippers faster, less costly alternatives to the canal, and the whole region began a long, slow period of decline.

But today, the towns and villages along the Erie Canal are enjoying economic resurgence thanks to the many tourists flocking to the area by land and water. Although the larger communities of Syracuse, Rochester, Schenectady, Rome, and Amsterdam have attracted some new industries, the renaissance along the canal seems particularly robust in smaller villages, with many restorations, museums, new restaurants, and numerous other improvements underway.

Little Falls, NY, has been largely restored to its 19th-century glory, and after exploring some of its charming streets, we stop at the Ann Street Deli & Restaurant for a relaxing lunch. This Canal City has a rich history and is full of architectural treasures, Revolutionary War monuments, and museums. The big canal lock at Little Falls, especially, is a must see. With a lift of 40.5 feet, it's the largest lifting lock on the entire New York State Canal System and one of the oldest.

Continuing west on SR 5, we pass through Utica, NY, and continue on to the north shore of Lake Oneida. Carved by glaciers during the last Ice Age, this lake is the largest used by Erie Canal traffic. Although we had planned to stop for an early dinner at the canal harbor in Brewerton, NY, rapidly building thunderheads in the west, convince us to make a dash for our hotel instead.

About an hour from Baldwinsville, NY, I discover that the shortcut I had mapped out on the spur of the moment was turning into a "longcut." By the time we make it to the Microtel in Baldwinsville, it's getting late and we're two very hungry travelers. We

Historic Skene Manor overlooks the Champlain Canal in Whitehall, NY.

all but throw our luggage into the rooms and hastily set off for dinner at the B'ville Diner. Over hearty homestyle vittles, I relate to Bruce that the town was originally settled by Dr. Jonas Baldwin, who relocated here from Maryland with his wife in 1808. They were Baldwinsville's first permanent settlers in this area of natural scenic beauty, which at that time was still very much on the American Frontier.

TO NIAGARA FALLS

Although there isn't a designated byway for motorists to follow along the Erie Canal, SR 31 west from Baldwinsville keeps us fairly close to the canal's path. The flatter topography and cultivated land stretching in every direction make it seem more like we're in the Midwest rather than western New York. The roads are pleasant, but the charming villages along this section of the canal are the main attraction. Because today's route more closely follows the path of the original Erie Canal, villages such as Lyons, Palmyra, Macedon, and others display attractive collections of 19th-century buildings that have become trendy shops and restaurants. A slight detour north on 31F, however, brings us to perhaps the fairest canal village of them all.

Thoroughly embracing canal-town atmosphere and culture, Fairport, NY is considered the "Jewel of the Erie Canal." Only 20 minutes from downtown Rochester, this is the one destination of our entire journey that spurs some wild thoughts about relocating.

Bruce and I take a walking tour to soak up every detail of this beautiful little village. Particularly intriguing is the "sloped" lift bridge over the canal, which is listed in *Ripley's Believe It or Not*. The innovative, double-walkway design of these bridges allows pedestrians to continue crossing over the canal even when the bridge is in its raised position.

The first use of the village's name of Fairport has been attributed to a traveler, who arrived in 1829 and deemed it a "fairport" in which to stay. On the north side of the canal, the Royal Café immediately grabs our attention as the perfect place to satisfy our ravenous appetites, and the excellent lunch had there is followed by an engaging conversation with the owner and another patron. They are eager to hear all about our travels along the New York Waterways.

The afternoon is filled with more attractive canal villages, including Brockport, Albion, Medina, and the not-so-small canal town of Lockport, NY. A stair-stepped flight of five locks here brought canal boats over the 75-foot-high Niagara Escarpment to the final leg of their water journey to Lake Erie. Although the original locks were later supplanted by two much larger modern locks, the original flight of five double locks' underlying stone structure was retained as a spillway. In a planned boost to tourism, Lockport is reinstalling wooden lock doors in their original positions on the flight of five locks. It should be quite a stunning visual treat, even if they're not in actual use with canal traffic.

SR 31 takes us the last few miles to Niagara Falls. Touring the New York waterways was an even more fulfilling experience than I had anticipated. And I especially enjoyed learning more about the history of the region and meeting so many warm and friendly people along the way.

62

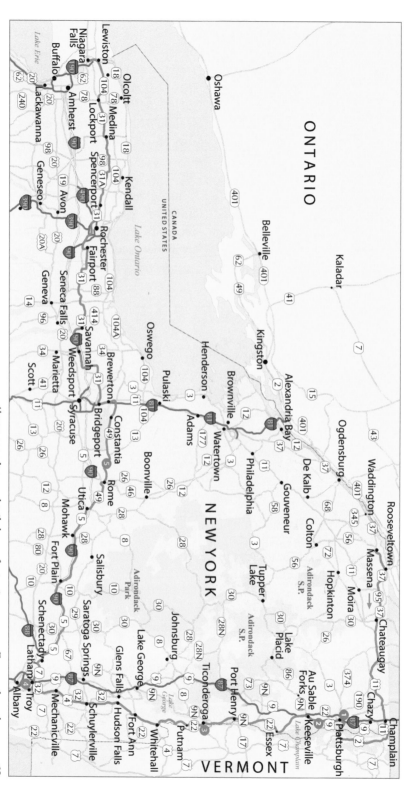

Always consult more-detailed maps for touring purposes. For map legend, see page 65.

FACTS & INFO

NEW YORK WATERWAYS

Approximately 652 miles

OVERVIEW

If you enjoy watching boats navigate canals and locks, touring historic sites, walking the streets of old, quaint townships, traveling amid beautiful scenery, and meeting friendly people, then this tour is for you.

Given my general preference for family-owned restaurants, I was pleased to find so many of them during this tour. Accommodations in the smaller towns along the route were limited in number. Consequently, reservations during the summer months are recommended. Most of the lodgings are either national chain motels of the one- or two-star variety, or modest family-owned establishments.

Although we allowed four days for the tour, we barely scratched the surface concerning the numerous sites along the way. For example, we didn't hike the trails in the Ausable Chasm, to explore the Cayuga and Seneca Canal or the Oswego Canal, or take a boat ride on the Erie Canal and stop at every interesting canal town we passed through.

ROADS

All of the roads on the route are generally well marked, have good pavement, and are just about perfect for laid-back touring at a moderate pace.

RESOURCES

- **New York State Canal System**
  www.nycanals.com
- **Fort Ticonderoga Events Calendar**
  www.fortticonderoga.org/calendar

POINTS OF INTEREST

1. **Lakes to Locks Passage**
   www.lakestolocks.org
2. **Ausable Chasm**
   www.ausablechasm.com
3. **Fort Ticonderoga**
   www.fort-ticonderoga.org
4. **The Mohawk Towpath Scenic Byway**
   www.mohawktowpath.homestead.com
5. **Erie Canal**
   www.eriecanal.org

Download the RoadRUNNER Rides app for turn-by-turn directions.

A collection of stories featured in

www.roadrunner.travel

RoadRUNNER Motorcycle Touring & Travel magazine is a bimonthly publication packed with exciting travel articles, splendid photography, route maps, and other features that help ensure wonderful two-wheeled adventures.

Subscriptions are available on www.roadrunner.travel and by calling (866) 343-7623,or by subscribing through the app store.

MAP LEGEND

ROADS/DESIGNATIONS

(12) U.S. Roads/Hwys

(12) Interstates

(12) State/County Roads

Route

Scenic Roads/Byways

Border

CITIES/POPULATION

○ Over 500,000
◉ 100,000 – 499,999
● 10,000 – 99,999
● 1,000 – 9,999
• Below 1,000

ICONS/MISCELLANEOUS

➝ Route Direction

1 Points of Interest

State Parks

Maps featured in this book are overviews of each roadtrip and are intended to be helpful guides. Always consult more-detailed maps for traveling purposes.

CPSIA information can be obtained
at www.ICGtesting.com
Printed in the USA
BVHW020458150620
581449BV00004B/117